Taco the Cat

By Chrystale Langford

Library For All Ltd.

Taco the Cat

First published 2023

Published by Library For All Ltd
Email: info@libraryforall.org
URL: libraryforall.org

Our Yarning logo design by Jason Lee, Bidjipidji Art

Original illustrations by Jovan Carl Segura

Taco the Cat
Langford, Chrystale
ISBN: 978-1-923063-04-4
SKU03367

Taco the Cat

There's a cat in our house.

MEOW.

He is a tabby cat.

MEOW.

We named him Taco.

MEOW.

Taco goes to our room.

MEOW.

9

He curls up to sleep
on the bed.

PURR, PURR.

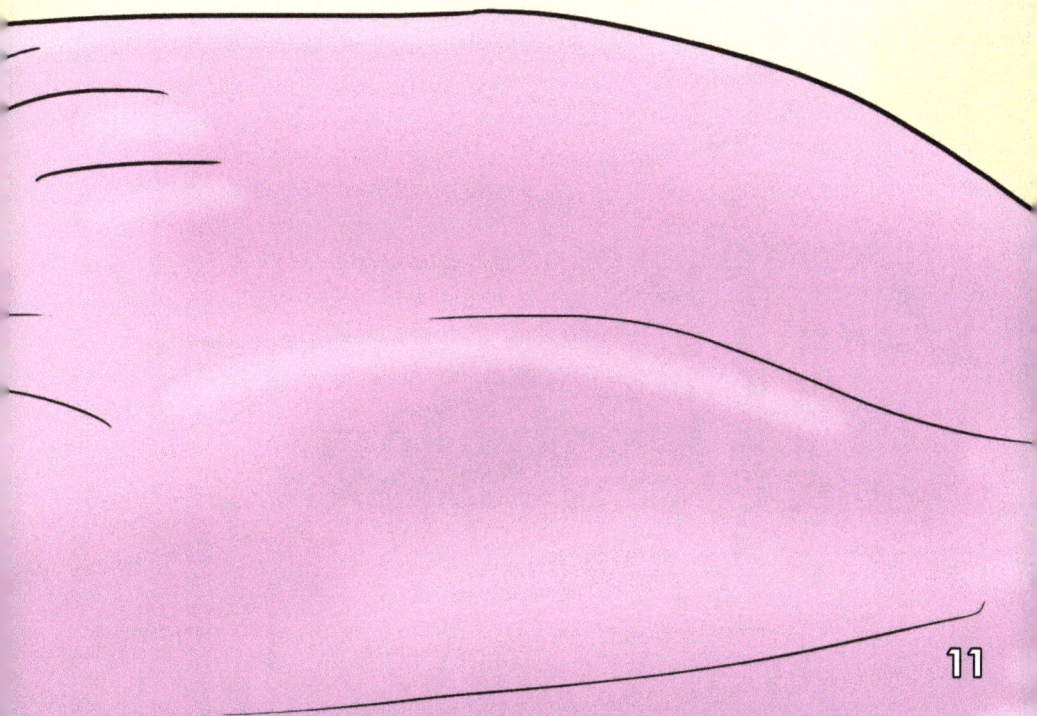

Taco likes pats
and cuddles.

PURR, PURR.

He is always hungry.

MEOW.

He is a skinny cat.

MEOW.

17

Taco is a happy cat.

MEOW, MEOW!

You can use these questions to talk about this book with your family, friends and teachers.

What did you learn from this book?

Describe this book in one word. Funny? Scary? Colourful? Interesting?

How did this book make you feel when you finished reading it?

What was your favourite part of this book?

download our reader app
getlibraryforall.org

About the author

Chrystale is from the Wiradjuri Nation and lives in Canberra with her children. She loves playing games together with them and having picnics. *Black Beauty* was her favourite book when she was young.

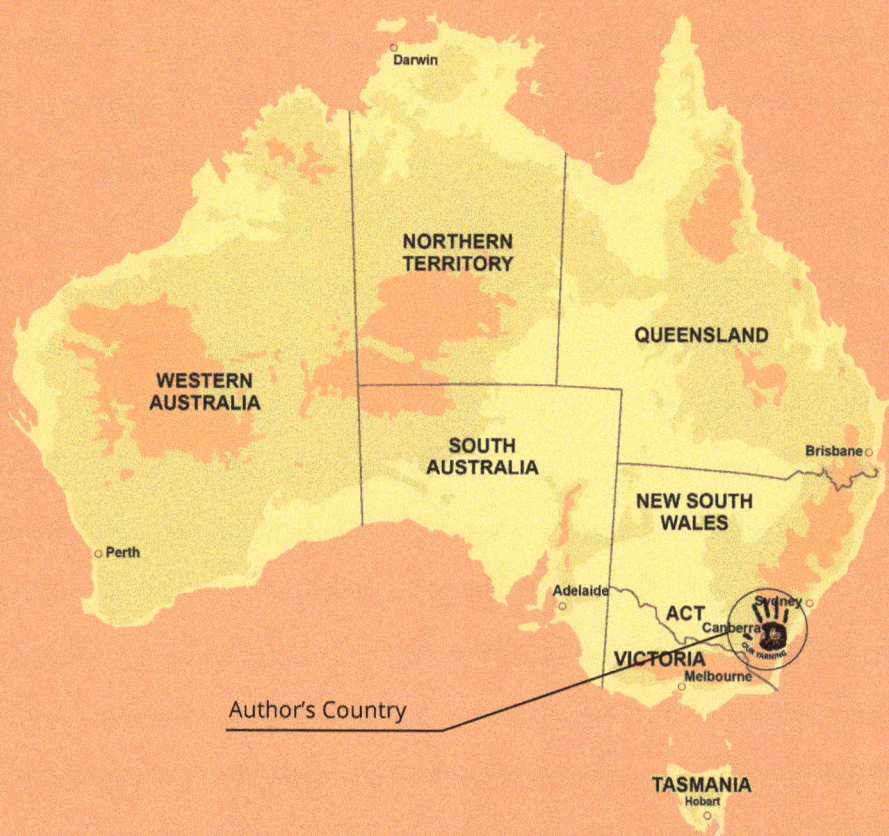

Darwin

NORTHERN
TERRITORY

QUEENSLAND

WESTERN
AUSTRALIA

SOUTH
AUSTRALIA

Brisbane

NEW SOUTH
WALES

Perth

Adelaide

Sydney
ACT
Canberra
OUR YARNING

VICTORIA
Melbourne

Author's Country

TASMANIA
Hobart

Our Yarning

Want to discover more books from this collection? Our Yarning is a collection of books written by Aboriginal and Torres Strait Islander peoples across Australia.

We know that children learn better, and enjoy reading more, when they see themselves in the stories, characters and illustrations of the books they read.

To download the app, visit the Google Play Store on any Android device and search 'Our Yarning'.

libraryforall.org

www.ingramcontent.com/pod-product-compliance
Lightning Source LLC
Chambersburg PA
CBHW042348040426
42448CB00019B/3454